Reflections

SHORT STORIES IN POEMS

Mable Green

My Greatest Love

My greatest love was when I found you
When I was younger I really did not have a clue.
Our love was always built on divine trust
It went without saying. It was a must.

At an early age I was young in denial and thought I knew it all
But when you came into my life I knew I would not fall.
Heart ache after heart ache I had in the past
As a teenager I was definitely flip and too fast.

After losing so many people in my life
I thought I needed to stop and think twice.
One day I decided to give up all my fights
And go ahead and dedicate myself to you with all my might.

Love is strong whether you admit it or not
Once you commit all you have it really is hard to stop.
My life is so much better really it is true
I would be lost "*God*" if it wasn't for you.

Mom and Dad

Precious memories of you we hold so dear
Your prayers and stories were beautiful to hear.
Hugs and kisses we did embrace
All while you were living in *God's* good grace.

Missing you each day we really do
Our hearts still ache for your tender love so true.
You taught us plenty about the bible and the holy land
Always trust in *God* and not in man.

All your precious words we have learned to be true
Even in death we will always love and miss you.

Stay Strong

Stay strong they say life is just temporary
And there is no need for you to worry.
Stay strong they say he will be among family and friends
There will be glory in the end.

Stay strong they say and don't be so heavenly burden
He just took the time to close his curtain.
Stay strong they say it's just another chapter
He has gone on to see his master.

Stay strong Jesus would say for he is
with me now and every day.
He was just a loan to us all anyway.
Stay strong Jesus would say I'm the first and the last
Before his death his confessions he did cast.

Stay strong Jesus would say and have faith
He will be in my arms as he takes his place.
Stay strong and wipe those warm tears
Just think I was the one who gave him those years.

Stay strong Jesus would say as he
took his last breath in defeat
Stay strong Jesus would say he
humbled himself before my feet.
Stay strong Jesus would say don't think twice
For I was the one who gave him life.

Stay strong Jesus would say cherish
each moment along the way
For you are not here on this earth to stay.
Stay strong Jesus would say "This too shall pass"
When it's all said and done you too will be with me at last.

Stay strong Jesus would say heartaches
will continue you see
Stay strong Jesus would say in my heart you will always be.
Stay strong Jesus would say live your life on this day
For I will be the one who will guide you all the way.

Stay strong Jesus would say no need to have any fear
Believe just believe that I've always been here.
Stay strong Jesus would say whether
you are in or whether you are out
Call me up whenever you are troubled or ever in doubt.

Stay strong in your life's fight
It will be your time to be humble when you see the light.
Stay strong stay strong Jesus would say
"Trust in me for I am the light and I am the way".

The Old Man

Humped over in distress
He tempted to get dressed.
Problems with his back and his knees
Going outside for sure he would freeze.

For him alone no children came to see
It was just my dog Hunter and me.
I was only 9 years old
But I felt sorry for the old sole.

The weather was really cold near zero
3 degrees says the weather man on the radio
Caught him by his right hand
I wasn't sure about his plan.

He hopped along nice and slow
Carefully he was in the slippery ice and the snow.
He opened the door to his truck
Wouldn't you know he was in luck.

My father walked up and said
Don't bother I'll drive you Mr. Fred
Glad to have your boy around he told my dad
We teach him to love and help others my dad said.

The Drinker

Sitting here all alone
With my liquor bottle dry as a bone.
It was out of the question to walk to the bar
It is entirely way too far.

Time is now a little after five
I was told don't drink and drive.
Refuse to be a drinking jerk
Drive anyway and get someone hurt.

I walked to the nearby liquor store
So I could purchase some more.
We sold out of your alcohol brand
No more for you said the man.

Weather was cold and I was chilled to the bone
I was feeling sorry for myself and all alone.
Finally ran across a sick old man a perfect stranger
You keep drinking and you will be in danger.

Appreciating my sister's love and support
My drinking habits landed me in court.
There I was in such sorrow
Promising myself I'll quit tomorrow

The courts ordered me to get some help for myself
Just before my sister and I left.
Can't understand why I am in this mess
Maybe "*God*" is putting me through this test.

Nature

Sitting by the beautiful waterfall
I was thinking of nothing and nothing at all.
Listening to the birds that sing
It was on a bright and warm day of spring.

Butterflies yellow blue and brown
Spreading their beautiful wings around.
Admiring the beauty of the flowers and trees that bloom
A sure sign that summer is coming soon.

Today is here. And tomorrow will be gone
It is not promised to us and we may be alone.
Weather changes and seasons does too
Enjoy these nature gifts that has been provided for you.

A Time to Remember

In my 5th grade year in 1962
A young boy's life changed and mine did too.
At the precious and tender age of ten
He came to the country and moved in.

Yes mother and dad took him under their wing
Admiring him as they watched from our porch swing.
We ran and played hide-n-go seek
For my friend it was a wonderful treat.

Together we played marbles and jumped rope
He didn't want to go back to the city so he hoped and hoped.
In August school started and without a fuss
Together he and I boarded the big yellow school bus.

His face was shining like a brand new penny
Rather tall dark handsome and skinny.
In this small old school he was in
He found new girls and boys as friends.

After school we played basketball with an old tin can
Ball made of old socks and rags we were each other's fan.
He played hard and thought he was bad
Even when I beat him he didn't get mad.

Time passed fast so it seems
Before we knew it we had reached our teens.
Playing checkers around the heater and the old lamp
Poor we were. Could barely afford a three-cent stamp.

Then one day in the middle of the night in October of 1965
Mother became ill and we all cried.
Turn out the light I said to my dad.
With a reply mother had a stroked and he sounded so sad.

We called the doctor and my sister too
My friend and I cried. There was nothing the doctor could do.
In the ambulance to the hospital mother went
24 hours around the clock we all had spent.

On the third day the doctor said
I will have to pronounce your mother dead.
When all the cars and siblings returned home with the news
One of us had to tell dad so we had to choose.

In mother's bedroom we gathered around our dad
Then my sister had to tell him the news that she had.
Grabbed and rubbed his chest with such pain
Why dear "God" didn't you take me it just won't be the same.

After the funeral everyone had to depart
Begin a new life without mother we all had to start.
Days weeks and months came and gone
We told ourselves tomorrow tomorrow will go on.

A couple of years later my friend began to date
Short tall couldn't make up his mind for goodness sake.
Not to be out done finally I found someone to date too
No one old but someone young and new.

After I graduated school I moved away
My friend and I had seized each moment every day.
We remembered how we played together
as children back then
I vowed separation and distance he
would always be my friend.

We had fun and heart to heart talks over the years
Yes together we shed many tears.
Even though I had left the country with all I had
Except my dear friend he stayed with dad.

Miles and miles away I would not be living near
Missing the laughter and long stories I no longer would hear.
Packed my bags and refused to look back
Remembering him the way he was as a matter of fact.

Drove away in the beautiful country sunset
Thinking of the first day on the farm where we first met.
Can't turn back the hands of time
All I had was memories of him in my mind.

Maybe one day before it's too late
We will meet again maybe by fate.
No more time to play our childhood game
So I married and took on another's name.

My friend graduated later and moved to the big city
He married and divorced. What a pity!
I learned we both each had two boys and a girl
What a coincidence: only in this world.

Then one day he heard I wasn't feeling well
Footsteps upon my porch came with a ring of my doorbell.
There he stood tall still handsome as ever
Childhood memories we shared forget them oh' never.

I thought many times to visit his place
Just to have a look upon your face.
He was supposed to only live with us for a while
Thought of him not only as our teen years
but when he was just a child.

Yes we played together as children back then
And became even closer when mother's
death gave us that spin.
Even though I have lost my father and my mother
I will forever love and remember my friend like no other.

The Rooster and the Cash

Our deacons and our preachers
They were always the good teachers.
Some said one thing and did another
Made promises and lied to their brother.

Says go on before it's too late
And put your money in the collection plate.
Instead I planted my money under the ground
So it could not be found.

Our old rooster found the stash
He pecked and pecked until he ate up the cash.
The rooster I decided to have for dinner
He was an old money eating sinner.

Later that day we did invite
My money chasing preacher was coming to eat that night.
As we begin to pray
The preacher looked over towards my way.

He says it is better to give than to receive
He ate the entire rooster. I do believe.
One thing about my little stash
The old preacher finally got my cash.

Sweet Irene

Sweet sweet wonderful Irene
She met a man years ago of her dream.
There she lived in the country of France
Meet the man of her dream was there a chance?

Tall dark and handsome a man she would adore
He was a soldier in uniform from the war
A good looking Englishman ready to wed
Marry sweet Irene before I am dead.

He called her up by telephone
Meet me sweet Irene as the radio played their song.
Took her in his long strong arms
Held her close until it was dawn.

They looked into each other's eyes
Until sweet Irene began to cry.
Be still my heart my handsome prince has come
Oh! Marry me marry me my sweet
Irene so we can become one.

They moved to the country of the U.S.
Sweet Irene opened a store where she was blessed.
Music he so often played
With his violin it was Irene he would serenade.

Then one day out of the clear blue sky
Her prince got sick and went on to die.
He left poor Irene to live by herself
She had no one no one else.

Even at the age of ninety seven
She still misses her prince up in heaven.
One day soon my darling prince you will see
Together together again we will be.

A Voice

Little old lady lying in bed
With her covers over her head.
Softly breathing while sound asleep
Very light breaths not very deep.

Not a chair or sofa she chose
Her bed her bed everyone knows.
No energy no fight for the day
Her bed her bed she would stay.

Confused depressed and lonely day and night
Lost her will to go on and fight.
Dampen by age and the loss of her man
Always speaking of seeing him again.

A voice came to her and said
Get up get up lady from that bed.
Live your life to its fullest and then
Think of seeing him not now but in the end.

Be Still

Looking over the meadows stream
Lonely forever as it though seems.
Heart so sad and filled with grief
Thinking of my lost just last week.

My headaches and my heart does too
Again and again as I think of you.
Be still my heart as I pray
You will come back to me someday.

My Friend

In the big windy city I was in
I came across a man. I called my friend.
I checked my watch. I thought I had broken
When he said hello so softly spoken.

In early November the weather was cold
I worked in a store with diamonds and gold.
The place was warm and quiet on that day
When he said I drove in from miles away.

He was well built as I could see
A date he wanted to have with me.
Without knowing even his name
I was very glad that he came.

Dressed in a white shirt and blue jeans
He was everything in my dreams.
Big smile he had on his face
No wrinkles no gray hair not even a trace.

He ask if I would go out on a date
Then promised he wouldn't be late.
I didn't want to be too nice nor too mean'
The answer was yes before he split the scene.

My bell rang at a quarter to seven
One look at him I thought I was in heaven.
He smelled good and dressed so nice
No way I had to think twice.

Off to the restaurant we went to eat
I even looked down at his feet.
Nice shoes expensive they appear
From his voice you look radiant my dear.

I've dated a lot of younger men
But that was way back when.
Even he drove from miles away
We both were happy on this day.

Precious Memories

As a child obey you were told
As parents we take on a different role.
Your ideas might not be the same
Why scar a good family name.

Even though you reached for the door
And you asked the question what in the world for?
So you decided after all to stay
And made a child happy on that day.

You remained within your parenting bound
Wondering where the correct answers to be found.
Be oh so careful my dear
Children judge by what they see and hear.

Set an example for the child you raise
Later in life they may give you the praise.
All the treasures of the pure gold
Cannot match the love they will hold.

In your life make the right choice
In the end you can rejoice.
Go beyond and above
Give them your time and your love.

You will pray with all your will
When you learn your child is ill.
When you approach the side of their bed
Tears of sadness you will shed.

Children grow up and get old
Precious memories they will hold.
Time will come and time will go
It could be over before you know.

When you have ran life's race
Think of tomorrow who will you face?
Time spent with that buddy or friend
Will never replace your child in the end.

War

To another war our soldiers were sent
It was by another one of our United States Presidents.
Military soldiers following his instructions
Over an unaccountable mass destruction's.

Back and forth Iraq and U.S. played tag
Until the Iraq leader was killed and we planted our flag.
Yes they were sent over to the enemy line
To fight an endless war that's been one of a kind.

So the U.S President took out the
Iraqi Leader Saddam Hussien
He was known all over by his name.
Tormented killed men women children and such
Showed no mercy compassion or love much.

Many of us dream of world peace so we can sleep
War after war our world seems to repeat
Waiting and wishing for the war to be complete
We better pray to "*God*" that our souls will keep.

Release Me

We promised to always be the best of friends
Until our lives come to an end.
We would not let each other down
And defend each other when someone else was around.

We would laugh often and sometimes too much
Tell sad stories cry and such.
We never treated each other as if we were dirt
We would give until it would hurt.

Our friendship was like honey sweet and thick
Then one day you got really sick.
And I remember those kind words you once have spoken
Our chain we have will remain unbroken.

Let's live life as if it is our last
It will go by ever so fast.
Even though my life won't be the same
I'd rather release you than see you suffer in pain.

Hanging Out

Hang with me Terry in our old hood.
I would Sean if I could.
Hanging out at my college dorms
Studying and filling out my school enrollment forms.

Hanging in the streets is not that cool
I'm staying in college and I'm no fool.
Come on Terry you're my old home-boy
Don't play me. I am not your toy.

Get out of the streets Sean it's not that safe
Come on and hang with me at my place.
Don't live your life in humiliation
Join me and get your education.

Sean one of my greatest fears
Where will I be in 10 years?
Terry man maybe the streets ain't for me
Maybe education is the key.

I'll sign up too for a class
And put this street thing in the past.
So what the guys will miss us man
But at least we'll have our future planned.

Baby Boy

Born as the last child of our family
You meant the world to your dad and me.
Seven solid pounds and all boy
You gave us such a great joy.

Through the house you'd pull up and fall
Dad said "He will play baseball."
As time went on and you became a teen
You filled your dad's dream.

He bragged and said it loud
A great pitcher you were and we were proud.
After you finished your high school
You decided to follow the family's rule.

Off to college you traveled to a near state
Because your future you had at stake.
Later you decided to follow Uncle Sam's rule
And two years later you left your college school.

Who would know what the future holds
When our time comes and our time goes
We don't know what our future will be
All we can do is depend on thee

Bill

Promises we made that after we died
We'd see each other on the other side.
We were together through thick and thin
Then one day he disappeared like the wind.

Wondered off without a trace
I prayed and prayed and kept the faith.
He left without even a trail
We were old and very frail.

Later on the news I saw
Was my friend old Bill Shaw.
It was then I made a telephone call
When I learned he had taken a fall.

We lived in a senior's home
When Bill decided he would roam.
Thank you "*God*" that he was all right.
It was the prayer I prayed that night.

Rainbow

Whatever will be will be
Because it comes from "*God*" you see.
He made the clouds and the sun
Man cannot undo what he has done.

He made the vegetables and the tiny seeds
The shade we enjoy from his trees.
He made the waters from all around
He made all of the beautiful sounds.

He made a flower of a different bloom
He made the day and the moon.
He made us humble when he began
He made us to be obedient and without sin.

God made people like the rainbow
Different colors and beautiful you know.
Each color can represent a different race
Each with beauty and no one can take its place.

When *God* sowed the human seed
He knew what he wanted indeed.
With his hands he made Adam first
Eve was his companion here on earth.

Yes he made rainbows with a different color
This is why we should love one another.
He made the eagle and the doves
He made man whom he loves.

Pass Me

Pass the bacon pass the eggs and the cheese
Pass the toast and pass the jelly please.
Pass the biscuits and pass the ham
Pass the grits and pass the jam.

Pass the beef and pass the greens
Pass the rolls and pass the beans.
Pass the chicken and pass the macaroni & cheese
Pass the stuffing and pass the peas.

Pass the salad and pass the tomatoes
Pass the turkey and pass the potatoes.
Pass the plate pass the fork and the knife
Pass the spoon and thank your wife.

Thunder

Across the meadows way over yonder
Rode my beautiful black horse old thunder.
Troubles and problems no one else had a clue
Get away get away I wanted to do.

Jumped from my horse onto the grass
Watching the large white clouds go pass.
Enjoying the butterflies on the wild flowers
Lying quietly there for hours and hours.

Feeling the light summer's breeze
Birds were flocking into the tall trees.
Dreaming of all my troubles away
It was on this gorgeous warm summer's day.

Old Friends

Two old guys of a different race
Sit down to talk face to face.
They had been friends for a very long time
And had different of opinions this was no crime.

They were always joking and kidding around
This day they headed towards downtown.
Will you tell me something old Joe?
Why do people hate each other so?

It brought Art eyes to tears
I don't know I tried to figure this out for years.
We should try to look inside a person's heart if you can
Because the color of the skin just don't make the man.

Why can't people be like us?
Enjoy life and not make a fuss.
People do crimes and go to jail
Why can't they love each other before they end up in hell?

Buck wild

Married we were to each other
Now you see life is a struggle.
Children of two you already had
They were cheerful and not at all sad.

No you had to eat all of your cake
Now you see it was a mistake.
All things together we would share
But you had decided to have an affair.

Out of this affair came a child
After you ran the streets and acted buck wild.
Even though your girlfriend already knew
You were married with children of two.

My hurt and distrust are with you not with the lady
It is not the fault of this baby.
I will have to think this over for a while
But divorce I'm thinking I may just file.

Judge said I respect you and you respect me
And visitations for the children it must be.
The only way I could ever have you still
It had to be through "God's" greatest will.

What's My Name?

We became friends when we met
Without me I made you sweat.
Let me make one thing clear
Listen carefully please do hear.

I can make you think you can fly
All while you are getting high.
Don't care if you are white or black
My name is old crack.

I can affect the way you breath
I can bring you to your knees.
On any month week or day
I can take all your works pay.

I can run through your big blue veins
I can make you have no kind of shame.
I can make you hang from the highest rope.
One of my name's is old coke.

I can mess with your head
And make you wish you were dead.
Now let me be real blunt
My name is a cigarette joint.

I can come in another mix
Whenever you need a good fix.
Who cares if you can't pay your bill
My name is deb the pill.

We all can make you forget your mother
We can take your only brother.
We can make you give up all your hope
We are still a form of dope.

Life Chances

There comes a time in every man's life
He will most likely seek him a wife.
A companion that will be willing to share
All his days he has to spare.

Along came sweet Betty Jean
The best looking woman I've ever seen.
Brown hair brown eyes with a nice frame
Now this is what I call a dame.

Good morning miss! On this lovely day
It is a pleasure to meet you I must say.
They call me big John
Don't be afraid I mean you no harm.

Your smile is warm and as beautiful as the sun
Would you like to enjoy this day with old John?
I would be delighted when my work is done
And enjoy this day with you and have some fun.

How would you like to walk in the park?
This could be a nice place to start.
I waited for a while and hoped it would be soon
Fell in love when she arrived that afternoon.

A red rose "please allow me to give"
I want you to know how I feel.
If you would allow me to speak out loud
I've been admiring you in the crowd.

When I drove up in my car
I would watch you from afar.
A woman likes a gentleman to be desired
You were one to be admired.

They met several times after that day
At her house she asked me to stay.
She gave me a kiss to show me she cared
About all our precious moments we had shared.

I don't want to be too forward or too blunt
But I need to get to the point.
I need only one woman you see
And I need that woman to need me.

Life is short and I don't need to think twice
Would you consider some day becoming my wife?
Yes time is short just like life
I would be happy to make that sacrifice.

Bank Day

On Tuesday as I walked into the bank
A mask man I thought I would faint.
He looked over at me with those dark eyes
As I listened to the other people cry's.

I knew I had to stay calm
And I couldn't walk away or run.
There I sat in my wheel chair
I knew the robber didn't care.

Unlike the others he didn't get in my face
He kept moving in a very fast pace.
I knew he was running out of time
When the banker gave me a sign.

I think he knew who I was
Don't ask how just because.
He watched every move I made
As we caught each other's gaze.

When he spoke a voice before I had heard
It was the old high school nerd.
This appear to be his first time I predict
When I figured out it was old Rick.

Beginning to slow his walk
I moved closer and begin to talk.
Get out now before the cops come
While you have the time to run.

Go ahead and get in your car
No one knows who you are.
Just as the cops walked in
He looked at me with a little grin.

He was wrong and showed no pride
This was when the cop's put him into their ride.
Happy we survived this scary day
As the cops took Rick away.

Adoption

Sitting in the dark all alone
Hoping this would not be my home.
Lights out early says old lady Blair
Sometimes she gets in my hair.

All the children looking mad
I try not to look so sad.
Visitors would come and visitors would go
Every time the answer would be no.

Would I get adopted? I had my doubts.
Everyday couple's came in and out.
They drove nice cars and even a Rose Royce
But I could never be their choice.

Then one day a young woman came
Tall beautiful and had a cane.
Wearing a warm and pretty smile
Could I ever become her little child?

Looking out at the water and the land
Then she reached out to hold my hand.
Dear child would you like to go for a walk?
This way we can have a nice little talk.

She told me I was as beautiful as the blue sky
Then I dropped my head and begin to cry.
She kneeled down at my little feet
Put her arms around me so soft and so sweet.

No one had said or done this before
I wanted to hear more and more.
Speaking softly I like you my dear
There's no reason for you to fear.

Go home with me she did insist
Finally my life had a new twist.
A real home at last is a good start
I will be forever grateful to her with all my heart.

Sins

Patty was my next door neighbor
She came over for a favor.
Lynne you were out last night at the bar
Come go to church with me it's not very far.

I cannot wear high heel shoes
Always wore flats even when I was in high school
Put on this new pretty white skirt
When we get there I'll fill you in on the dirt.

After we left the class of our Sunday school teacher
We began to wait for the church's preacher.
He took so dog gone long
They had the choir to sing another song.

From way in the back came this little chick
She read the scripture and trying to be slick.
A song she sang "Beam of Heaven as I Go"
Thought to myself oh yea down to hell below.

There's the first lady carrying the good book
The chick in the choir was the church cook.
Girl can you see where I'm going with this?
Yea things at the bar can't top this gossiping list.

Where is your preacher I want to know
He's not only late he is entirely too darn slow.
How would you know you never met him.
I don't have to look what he is carrying.

Straight from the kitchen
He walked in with a breast of chicken.
And wouldn't you know a chunk of cake
Then he had the nerve to be late.

Finally he spoke on all kinds of sin
I wondered if he actually listened within.
Maybe last night I was in the street
But isn't it a sin to over eat?

Preacher can eat all his chicken cake and pie
He better stop all that eating or he will die.
I might have had my smoke and my drink
But it is time for me to stop and think.

I know it is not good to slang mud
For us all "*God*" will be the last to judge.
I could be Cindy, Sue, or even Sam
What's important is who I am.

Thanks to Patty for taking me to church that day
I certainly have learned how to pray.
Now I can take in a great big sigh
And thank the "Almighty" from up high.

A Poem to Granny and PaPa

Roses are red. Violets are blue
You do so much for me
And I love you.

I know "*God*" put you here on earth
To love and teach me
Even before my birth.

So please continue to teach me
How to be a success
All my dreams will come true
And it will be because of you.

By: Mi'ya Terry-age 10

Future Goals

Start now and set your goal
Do not continue to wait to be told.
Look ahead towards your destination
Do it now without any further hesitation.

Build and build for your future things
You never know what planning brings.
Fall will pass and winter will too
Summer's gone and so will the spring's morning dew.

Don't sit there as if you have nothing to do
You never know who will be waiting for you.
Look up and make plans for your future at last.
Look back someday and see how far
you've come from the past.

Color of Darkness

I just do not understand
What it is about my race
And the color of my skin
Outside surface is not who I am within.

So I speak a language
That you cannot understand
Come from another country
But I am still a man.

Why put me in a group
That others want to keep away
My race was not by my choice
That I can change at the end of the day.

Why should we single other people out?
We know this isn't right
Because what's done in the dark
Will for sure come to the light.

We are the color of a beautiful rainbow
That can be found throughout our nation
When all colors are blended together
We're the beauty of "Gods" creation.

Stop and think and take the time
You can make a change
God created us all
And he made everyone the same.

Cowboy

Spread my blanket under the shade tree
It was just my picnic basket my dog and me.
Enjoying the beautiful Saturday afternoon
I was admiring the wild flowers with yellow blooms.

As I looked across the grassy field.
Up rode this cowboy named Bill.
He looked at me and began to say
Enjoying this quiet and warm beautiful day?

The closer he got the better he looked
When I offered him some food I had cooked.
Usually he didn't ride over this way
But he was glad on this beautiful day.

He thank me for the food and was about to go
Call me sometime he wanted to know.
Our picnic was over at this time
No way I would turn down a cowboy this fine.

In The Mist of the Storm

Falling down on both of my knees
I begged my dear "*God*" to please.
Spare this man his life
This is not the first time but twice.

The first storm was by mail
He did wrong and went to jail.
Out with his buddies having fun
When he was caught carrying a gun.

Time in jail was well spent
Where he made promises and repent.
Walked away a free man
When he begin to make his next plan

Started the wind hail and rain
This was when a real storm came.
I pray that you give him another try
Before I lay down and die.

Where were you?

Came a knock on my door
Stood a man I've never seen before.
He looked sick and rather sad
Hello son I'm your dad.

Church bell ringing in my ear
Time was really getting near.
I traveled all of this way
Give you my blessings on this day.

Where were you when I needed you the most?
In another country not very close.
Even though I was miles away
You were with me every day.

At age 3 when I broke my leg you weren't there
It did not mean son that I did not care.
Where were you when I cried in the night?
You were in my heart son just out of sight.

Where were you when school was about to start?
Son you were here in my heart.
I needed you dad when I was young
Let me be with you on this day my son.

As the piano began to play
I'm sorry son I'll just get out of your way.
I'm blessed today to be marrying my beautiful wife
And I am finally going to have you dad in my life.

7 Days a Week

Sitting here in a daze
I was day dreaming and planning my next few days.
Monday I'll start nice and slow
Tuesday will be here before you know.

Wednesday will be the middle of the week
The closer it gets I will not be able to sleep.
Thursday comes and the weekend will almost be there
Friday's work week will be over I declare.

Saturday night I will go out on my date
I'll go out but cannot stay too late.
Sunday morning I will speak those words from my lips
Time has come for my much needed trip

I Am

I am slim trim and mean
I can be your worse dream.
I can go near and far
I can live in your car.

I am in your kid's school
I can make them look real cool.
I am there when you play cards
I am on your church's yard.

I come in many styles
I can kill you after a while.
I might set in a tray
I might make your day.

I can come through your nose
I can get in your clothes.
I can go out in the air
I can linger in your hair.

I can go in a pipe
I can keep you up at night.
I can turn your insides black
I can bring on an attack.

I might help control your weight gain
I can cause you so much pain.
I can affect your tongues
I can collapse your lungs.

I am silent make no sound
I don't need you around.
I can make you not be the same
Old smoking tobacco is my name.

Stand Up

Men men take a stand
Show the world that you are a man.
Do not wait to be told
Be the man of your household.

It is not about getting a free ride
By all means show that you can provide.
Your wife should be able to depend on you
And your precious child does too.

Stand tall and be firm
Set examples for your children to learn.
A good message you will send
Stand up and be proud men.

Hitch Hiker

It was on a cold rainy day
I had spent all of my pay
Body cold and needed a ride
Up went my thumb from my side.

Trucks and cars going pass
Finally someone stopped at last.
A young man about 17 years old
Said "Get in I know you are cold.

I got in on the passenger's side
I took a deep breath before we began to ride.
We did not get very far
This was when he offered me a chocolate bar.

He looked a little wired up
And he kept drinking from his cup.
Let me say this real plain
I did not want to know his name.

I said to myself wait a minute
This kid is way over the speed limit.
He was doing 90 miles per hour
This is when my bladder lost its power.

Ready to get out mister just name the spot
Kid you can drop me off at the very next stop.
My forehead was sweaty and my hands were too
Pants were wet and so was my shoe.

Exited the car from the passenger right front
Then the kid offered me a cigarette joint.
The next time I decide to hitch hike
I'll flag down a kid on a bike.

The size of a Man

It's not the size that makes the man
Realize it when he holds your hand.
Before you go and make up your mind
He might be gentle sweet and kind.

Maybe he doesn't do that one special thing
Like bring you a diamond ring.
Maybe he'll send you a bouquet of roses
And has as much faith as our dear Moses.

Maybe he goes down on his knees
Or do not like a woman who wears a weave.
Please do not think of going off the hook
He might like a woman that knows how to cook.

We all have some type of faults
Whether it's lying cheating and never gotten caught.
It's some good in all of us
All we need to do is just have a little trust.

He might not be all you want him to be
But if he is in your life he is special you see.
So do not get all over stressed
You never know when you'll be blessed.

Thirteen

I was born and raised in Tennessee
Where I had friends that were poor like me.
Coming from a family of thirteen
A lot was lacking if you know what I mean.

I would go to school with a dress made from a flour sack
Owned one pair of slippers in the color of black.
My hair was combed in two braids
My mom and dad I have to give them the praise.

We walked a half mile for the school bus
And we tried not to complain or make a fuss.
Every day I had peanut butter and crackers for lunch
From the looks of others I had a whole bunch.

In the winter months they kept us warm
Keeping us loved were their charm.
Some days it was a great big deal
There were days for this family to have a full course meal.

When mom died at age fifty two
I was thirteen and didn't know what to do.
Dad raised me until I was grown
He prayed that nothing would go wrong.

Many days I saw and felt his pain
And tears I barely could contain.
Mom and Dad you can't compare
Because men and women are different it wouldn't be fair

Sometimes I felt that he was a little out of touch
But he showed me he cared so very much
Firm and out of touch he may have been
If I could only have that love now as back then.

I remember his laughter and his jokes
We were told to keep up our hopes.
Sure he liked to have good clean fun
Dad taught us your word is your bond.

When it came to work foolishness he set aside
Always setting good examples was his guide.
When he passed he was seventy three years old
His love and memories I will forever hold.

A Young Man's Story

This story I must tell
Years ago I was put in jail.
As they say you do the crime
You also must do the time.

This here is the real scope
I went out and I sold dope.
I also stole several cars
And then I ended up behind bars.

When I found out who turned me in!
I knew it was no way I could win.
It was my wonderful and faithful wife
She said "I did it to save your life."

Sure I broke down and I cried
But help me I knew she had tried.
I did not care what people thought
Not until I had gotten caught.

Judge I know I made this choice
When I tried to raise my voice.
He said to me "as of this very date
You will remain behind the gate."

Think about getting your life together
Not just for you also for the other fellow.
Don't continue to make these same mistakes
Your family cares for you for goodness sakes."

I stood there with tears running down my cheek
I felt low and awfully cheap.
Yes I was feeling so ashamed
This is when I knew I had to change.

On good behavior I served five years
Let me tell you there weren't any thrills
At my sentencing my wife promised to wait
Sure enough there she stood in good faith.

I promised "*God*" when my time was done
I would be good and help everyone.
I continued to live my life straight
So I will never go back behind that gate.

Last Dance

There he stood handsome as ever
I've been watching this good looking Fellow.
He made his move across the floor
I stood up so I could see more.

He was definitely playing it cool
I could tell he wanted to make his move.
I saved him the trouble and walked over to him
The lights were nice and very dim.

Excuse me sir my name is Nell
He said "Please to meet you as well."
How do you feel about dancing with a lady?
Turn down a beauty like you I would be crazy.

As he took me by the hand
He says "by the way my name is Dan."
Well Dan you are a nice dancer I must say
Thank you Nell I'm glad you feel this way.

I felt so good in his arms
We danced and danced until it was dawn.
Thank you Dan for a wonderful night
He replied think nothing of it. It was a delight.

I come to this place now and then
Do you think that I will be able to see you again?
I looked at him as if I was in a trance
He said only if I could have the last dance.

In Marriage

In marriage there is no just you
You then become two.
In marriage there is no me
Me then becomes we.

In marriage togetherness you and me
You I and me changes you see.
In marriage aren't any I's but us
It is based upon love and trust.

In marriage looking for other places to be
It is based on two people not three.
In marriage there is no weakness to lust
Love communication and honesty is a must.

Do not let someone else help you do your dirt
This way no one else will get hurt.
In marriage stay clean in order for it to work
You made vows before "*God*" in the church.

Classmates

Jenny and Davy met at the mall
She was short and he was tall.
Did not get involved because of his plans
No harm done just being a responsible man.

Last year they were classmates
And they had a couple of dates.
She talked about her future ideas
Included going away bringing her to tears.

Are you making your future plans Davy?
I'm not sure yet but I thought of joining the Navy
When I finish my last high school course
I will most likely join some type of military force.

Maybe the arm force will be where I'll serve
Then life threw him a nice little curve.
Few months later he learned that he had a tumor.
This was a fact and not just some rumor.

He asked the Doc is there any way this is treatable.
The Doc replied it is also removable.
No reason to change plans as far as I can tell
Go ahead son and serve your country well.

Face to Face

Our most gracious father while you hold my hand
Guide my feet through this precious land.
Held my head up high
As I continue to look to the sky.

Protected me through my daily flights
You comforted me through my sleepless nights.
There were days that I went astray
You guided me throughout each day.

To death ears confusion will bring
I'm a child of our most High King.
Times I went through some kind of phases
But continued to depend on you and gave you your praises.

Born on this beautiful earth
With you I seek a new birth.
Now a woman once a little girl
Soon be done with this old world.

Face to face we will someday meet
Humble myself before your feet.
Until then I will look to the heavens above
Thank you "Dear *God*" for all of your love.

The funeral

Thursday I pondered through the night
Wondering if I would make it until daylight.
Finally I drifted off to sleep
I was counting Billy goats and the sheep's.

Morning came with the beautiful yellow sun
I was wondering if everything' would be done.
Watered the garden and hung up the hose
I picked out my shoes and my clothes.

My hair was cut and my eyes were red
As I set on the edge of my bed.
Took another stiff drink as I got dressed
Stood up straight I tried my best.

I went to the car and started her up
Then I took another sip from my cup.
Drove down to the church on that day
Parked my car and begin to pray.

Lord I don't want to pass judgment on this guy
I know someday I'm going to die.
He was terrible beat his wife you see
Worse of a man than old drunken me.

All I've done was drink and party sometime
Even tore up my neighbor's property and even mine.
Walked in the church nice and slow
This is the man. I seem to know.

Shook my head from side to side
I'm not that drunk I know you died.
So I sit down next to him in the pew
He said the funeral is not for me but it's for you.

Every time I come you're not dead
You are sitting in this pew instead.
Picked up my hat let out a big sigh
See you next week since you won't die.

My neighbors

Tic Toc went the old clock
As I put on my last sock.
Out in the cold I had to go
I shoveled the deep six feet of snow.

When I started to dig
I heard the sound of a pig.
He had gotten out of his pen
Then up walked this man name Ben.

Cute little pig with his tail in a twist
He is just a pet and won't hurt you miss.
Help you! I can with your snow
I just live only next door.

We heard you moved in yesterday
Hope you have a wonderful stay.
I Plan to stay with any luck
Right now my vehicle is stuck.

Thank you kindly for your help!
This is when I started up my step.
What is that aroma I smell?
Homemade bread I can tell.

Wind chill is awfully cold you know
Come on in and have a cup of Joe.
He set in the big straight chair
And he even looked relaxed with not even a care.

Have you lived next door for long?
Live with my mother I'm not alone.
I have lived here all of my life
I haven't any children or even a wife.

I was young when I lost my dad
Heard he was a fine old lad.
Ben I never knew my mother
I looked years ago now I don't bother.

Looking down in my coffee cup
She had me young and gave me up.
She was about 15 born around 1942
Married and had a son too.

A picture of my mother I got from my dad
This was the only one he ever had.
Looking out the window across the fence
I've been looking for her ever since.

You probably haven't seen my mother before
But this picture looks like her next door.
Like us dark hair and rather tall
I will give her a telephone call.

A shadow I could see through the kitchen curtain
It was his tall mother for certain.
In she walked with a pot of stew
Says you don't know me but I know you.

Felt you in my heart for many years
Then we all ended up in tears.
I am your old long lost mother
And this young man is your brother.

Daughter I was young and foolish way back when
It doesn't matter mother. It was then.
All these years "you" I did not know
Just hold me tight and never let go.

Weight Loss

Daughter is playing with her new cat
While mother tries to lose her winter's fat.
Under the big coats the weight did not show
Twenty pounds more she has to go.

In winter she promised to diet
But her excuse I'm just too tired.
Thirty pounds over she went
I'll lose it just wait until Lent.

Clothes didn't fit because of those sags
Off to the gym she packed her bags.
So out to the car in a huff
I'll start today. It cannot be too rough.

Driving down the street called 7 mile
She got her phone and started to dial.
Girlfriend you better make your self-free
And come on and go with me.

There they were off to the gym
They stretched their tummies backs and their limbs.
Eat hamburgers and shakes we will not dare
Aches and pains we indeed had to share.

It has to be a better trick
Next time I will not eat myself sick.
I may now carry this frown
Next month I'll be the best looking chick in town.

The Flight

On a cold winter's night
I was waiting for my flight.
Seeming so eager to fly
Walked up this old guy.

Going to be with his only son
Sitting and waiting wasn't any fun.
He had a lot on his mind
He appeared not to have very much time.

He had a stroke a year back
As he held his little paper Sack.
I was hoping he was feeling okay
Learned his son died on Christmas Day.

He was in such a big rush
Getting there early was a must.
Sadness in his voice I could hear
Visited his son's grave the same time every year.

Trust me

I took care of you when you were a child
Even though you were sick once in a while.
Walked you to school on your first day
And I taught you how to pray.

I was up with you during the night
Remember tucking you in oh so tight.
I protected you from the bullies while you were in school.
Putting my arms around you even when you broke a rule.

Guided you throughout your teenage years
Consoled you and wiped away your tears.
It did not matter what you had
It did not matter how much you got mad

You are grown with a good start
I will remain in your heart.
I will be with you in your future days
Because I am "God" I will be with you always.

Respect

Respect your family
Who you know!
Respect your friends
Who you will show!

Respect your co-workers
Also your peers!
Respect those
You have worked with for years.

Respect each one
Of the human race
Respect them all
As you take your place.

Respect each man
And women alike
Respect them all
While they are still in sight!

Respect each other
As they deserve.
Respected by *God*
Who we do serve!

Sexy

As he set by the window enjoying the morning sun
Long before I take my morning run.
I called him Sexy because sometimes during the night
He would be no place in sight.

Around eleven O' clock I would retire
But going out at night was his desire.
He did not use the front door. He used the side
Every night he left and showed no pride.

I told him let's make a deal
If you are not back in time you get your own meal.
Well as years went by I stop showing my concern
Coming back on time he had to learn.

So I prepared his food and began to serve
Giving him a good meal I know he deserve.
Sure enough he came to the table and sat
Kitty's name was Sexy my old beautiful cat.

An Unforgettable You

He was off to hunt to kill a deer
When I had this awful fear.
Stay I would say the snow is too deep
Lately my dear you've been unable to sleep.

Walked out through the kitchen door
Loving and admired him more and more.
Kissed hugged said his "goodbye".
I best be strong and not cry.

Suns up now he'll be back soon
Way before we see the next moon.
Out the window I took that one last look
Finally I settled down with a book.

Strange thoughts entered my head
As I approached our big bed.
Hunters were shooting at their game
When suddenly I thought I heard my name.

Jumped up from across our bed
Off to the woods I fled.
Calling out his name Jim! Jim! Jim!
Hoping I could hear a sign from him.

Walked and followed his shoe tracks
Came across his two old big sacks.
Face down there he lay
With him I must stay.

Gunshots rang in the air
Oh "My *God* this isn't fair.
From my mouth came a scream
When up appeared two men on the scene.

They carried my husband back home
They said it wouldn't be wise to be alone.
For a while now he had been very sick
I hurried and called the doctor real quick.

Doctor came and was writing on his pad
Heart attack Miss's your husband has had.
Tears came as I fell to my knees
Bring him back oh *God* would you please?

All we had was each other
I cannot see myself going on any further.
Snow storms or whatever
We promised we would always be together.

Looking upon my husbands face
I accepted he lost life's race.
Kissing his lips I truly cried
I was feeling so very empty inside.

Remembrance of this sad day
I will always have to pray.
Life goes on this is a must
He is with Jesus whom I trust.

Homeless

I am homeless asking for money to spare
Yes I was in soup lines for the good people to share.
Searching near and so very far
Just to seek jobs no matter where they are.

An old man I met full of advice
I listen to him not once but twice.
He was fragile kind hearted and so very wise
His friendship I could not jeopardize.

As we watched people get out of control
He says "stressful times we hold".
I reminisced over my days past
Wondering how I got to this point so fast.

He said "Our homes and cars we have lost
And a pretty penny it did cost.
Times like these our minds will sway
We know it has to be a better day."

Old man I do not know how to feel
But I know it is all so real.
Maybe I cannot sleep in my old warm bed
I will be thankful to have any roof right now over my head.

Come with me under the bridge he say
Down here together we can stay.
Sorry young man we have no light
So I am saying to you have a goodnight.

I slept at ease until the next day
I realized my friend had slipped away.
I gathered my belongings and my few treats
I did not want to die in the streets.

Old man you had an awful lot of pride
I guess I'll see you on the other side.
Cold days and troubled times will be
But you my friend are now "Free".

Breaker Breaker

Breaker Breaker number nine
He was tall dark and oh so fine.
Approach him I would not dare
He looked as If he did not care.

Around the corner I saw him go
Drove his truck so carefully and slow.
As he looked the other way
I never thought I would see him again someday.

Days came and weeks past
I will see him finally at last.
June 2nd on the calendar I set
This was the date we had met.

After we went on our first date
Then I knew it wasn't too late.
He held me close and so very tight
I did not want to say goodnight.

We looked into each other's eyes
We stood there and said our good byes.
Watched him for the longest as he got back in his truck
I told myself this can be nothing but real luck.

He drove away with a sweet little grin
Says when I come back I'll see you then.
Even though we were apart
I loved him with all my heart.

The telephone rang. I nearly had a fit
His sexy voice I melted I must admit.
He said tomorrow I should be coming to town
I want to know if you would hang around.

Upon his return a small box he did bring
He asked "Will you marry me and accept this ring?"
I replied I loved you then and nothing has changed
I would be happy to have your last name.

Image

When you look in the mirror
Who do you really see?
I hope it is the image
That *God* meant for you to be.

Your eyes may be brown
Or like the daylight's sky
You will always be
An apple of his eye!

Days come when you feel
As though you are being used.
Know that you are beautiful
And do not have to be abused.

You may be homeless
And walk a pavement street
You are important
Not beneath anyone's feet.

People may say you are weak
And cannot keep up with the troubles of time
You are loving and strong
God says you are an image of mine.

Bow Down

Bowed down on my bending knees
And ask the lord if he would please.
Forgive me of all my sins
Not just outer but within.

Picked me up when I was down
And set my feet on solid ground.
Raised me up when I wasn't ready
Guided me and kept me steady.

Woke me up when I had no clock
You healed my body without the doc.
You've been good to all of man-kind.
You are never late always on time.

Fly Away

Twiddle Twiddle little bird
Your singing I have heard.
Wings flopped against your breast
As you nestle in your nest.

Beautiful feathers oh so blue
Danger danger is all around you.
Slick and sliding getting near
A snake is coming can't you hear?

If he strikes it will not be fair
Safety will come in the air.
So spread your wings as you were coached
Fly away fly away before he approach.

Up you go so very high
Safe you are in the sky.
When you land in a new place
You can thank *God* for his good grace.

Daughter Dearest

Daughter daughter I must say
You are special in every way.
You were the apple of your dad's eye
I was so happy. It made me cry.

Later came pitter patter of your little feet
You were a joy and a treat.
Teenage years came and time for prom
You wore such beauty and such charm.

Now that you are grown with children of two
They are a blessing for your husband and you.
Your children will fall in love and start to date
Guide them carefully for goodness sake.

When that day come for you to part
Just like your parents you will love
and keep them in your heart.
While there is time enjoy each and every day
Always remember you will need to pray.

My First Son

When you were born in the hospital that day
We knew you were special in every way.
Dad held you close. Your looks were the same
So I gave you his precious name.

Silently watching you play with your toy
You made me happy I had a boy.
Brown and beautiful my precious child
You were gentle and sweet with a beautiful smile.

As parents we set our house rule
You had to work or go to school.
Off to college you fled
You had good knowledge in your head.

After you finished all your college courses
You made your future choices.
A job you took as a boss
We could see school was not a total loss.

Moved forward with your success.
Because we knew you deserved the best.
One day a wife you will seek
Love and respect her when you meet.

As I watched you so meek and mild
Someday son you too will have a child.
Guide them when they start
Pray for them daily and keep him in your heart.

My Soldier

Son when I learned that you would serve overseas
The thoughts brought me to my knees.
Sunny days shined bright and clear
I find myself wishing you were here.

Even though last year has gone
I sit here all along.
Distance between us seem so far
Wondering just where you are.

Listening to the birds that sing
I'm thinking what tomorrow will bring.
You're my child the world can see
In my heart you will always be.

Silence a voice would say
You will see him again if you pray.
When all is said and all is done
My love and thoughts will remain with you my son.

Teamwork

Today we met with our boss
The company had taken a loss.
We have another budget to cut
We all wondered just how much.

On this day we had learned
There was a two million dollar cut was confirmed.
We were told If you do not want to be on a sinking ship
Let me just give you this little tip.

I knew this sounded like the same old song
But our department budget was twenty thousand along.
You all always were the best over achievers
And you have and are very good leaders.

We all have been around this block
Please keep in mind we were up against the clock.
There wasn't any need to get all worked up and nervous
This team has always given very good service.

On our deadline we made our budget goal
The big boss was pleased as we were told.
He bragged not only did you just deliver
You all gave so much of yourselves a true team giver.

Everything went smoothly without any complications
Thanks to my entire staff for all of their dedications.
All the hard work upon you I had to bring
I am proud to have such a wonderful and dependable team.

Proud

You fought in the military on the enemy line
Saving the lives of others all of that time.
Missing your parents spouse children and cousins
We watched our American soldiers killed by the dozens.

Back in America whom you protected
Get discriminated against and neglected.
How painful this must really be
To live among people that say we are free.

You served proudly in mud and rain
I wish the American people could feel your pain.
It must have been tough when you begin
And if you had to protect this country you would do it again.

Color Me

Color me color me the lightest or the darkest of the skin
It does not matter because I am the same within.
Color me color me does it really matter?
Color me color me is half of the battle.

Color me color me, the same as any race
It does not matter because I know my place.
Color me color me the same as the Irish descent
It does not matter because I am who *God* has sent.

Color me the color of the beautiful rainbow
It does not matter because *God* and I do know.
Color me the color of any race of all of mankind
It does not matter because I will be just fine.

Color me color me and give me that old special name
It does not matter because I will remain the same.
Color me color me for *God* made me from his beautiful earth.
It "DOES MATTER" because we do not
know who really came first.

A Senior Moment

I woke up this morning feeling just fine
Until I tried to use my mind.
I forgot to get out of bed
For a moment I thought I was dead.

I pulled my covers back
And I raised my head until I found out some facts.
My walker was across the room
As the clock chimed it was now noon.

I stood to my unsteady feet
In these old years I did not want to repeat.
My knees went wobbly and my arms weak
I fell back on the bed and took a seat.

It come a knock at the door
I keep seeing this man and do not want to see him anymore.
Suddenly a voice spoke are you alright my dear?
It was my doctor and my mind was clear.

Many times I just knew it was the undertaker
Thank goodness each time it was the good lord my maker.
The next time you have a senior moment
no need to cry even a tear
It is just a senior moment. There is no need to fear.

Slavery Time

You were born a slave and wanted to be free
At that time in the 1800's it wasn't meant to be.
Held back and used as a slave
Died and buried in your grave.

The hard times you suffered for your family
Denied freedom simply because master
did not want you free.
Family members and friends went through the same thing
Must have been hard to reframe.

Because of your sufferings abuse and more
You helped your children with suffering and opened a door.
So thank you Grandma and Grandpa
for all that you had to endure
Laying the ground work for your family for sure.

Search for Freedom

You were born as a slave in 1845
No place to run and no place to hide.
Came over on a boat with your father and your mother
Lived in Hornsby Tennessee and did not move any further.

Stayed in the country possibly in the sticks
Sold on an auction block at the tender age of six.
You met Grandma at an early age
Did not look back just turned the next page.

She was twelve and you were fourteen
Married each other because of the love in between.
Slavery must not have been any easier for either of you
But I am grateful you made it through.

So thank you grandma and Grandpa for what you've done
Setting things into place so this
generation does not have to run.

Born to be Free

You married Grandpa years ago
There were hard times and at times things were slow.
Sold eggs quilts and other goods
You did all you knew how whenever you could.

Took care of your daughters as they gave birth
You took care of them and them first.
To many of mothers you were a midwife
Bringing their children into this world and giving them life.

You were helpful to others throughout the land
Supporting them all and you did it for your fellow man.
Thank you for your love and your support
Thank you for everything for everything so much.

Freedom Rings

Slaves were freed in 1865
where you were maybe not Nation Wide.
You stood there at age three
Waved goodbye to your mom but was she really free?

Alone with your sister she was sixteen
Freedom had come for your family's dream.
You were able to vote when others could not
Went on to buy up land and you did not stop.

Put in knowledge labor and your devotion
Expecting it all to pay off without any commotion.
Made a way for your children before you were deceased
You left them in good shape May you rest in Peace.

The Trapper

You were the first born of mom and dad
Cool smooth and a handsome old lad.
Enjoyed the outdoors on our old farm
Learned that you were also quite the charm.

Hunted and trapped the rabbits and the coons
Not for long you left home so soon.
Traveled the roads to Detroit city
Learning your way at such young age what a pity!

As time went on we all joined you one day
Thank you my brother for leading the way.

Sister Dearest

My sweet sweet sister Idell
There's so much about you I would like to tell.
Kind hearted gentle and loving too
Gave your last if you had it this was so true.

Television car typewriter clothes and such
Letters telephone calls and visits how you kept in touch.
Even when you were feeling down you had a heart of gold
This was not something that I was told.

Stood in the hallway looking at you in your recovery room
Lose you then would have really been too soon.
You waved your hand motioning for me to come in
Speaking so fast on your recovery day back then.

Tell my sister to come and write my story
You wanted it told before going home to glory.
Yes you were special in so many ways
We will continue to miss you for days and days.

Somebody's coming

As momma and I sat under the shade tree
She was content as content could be.
At times she appeared to be in such deep thought
While I watched our dog and cat as they always fought.

After a while I heard a soft voice
It wasn't speaking to me but to *God* by choice.
Interrupt momma I would not dare
she was in such a deep deep prayer.

Up raised her precious little head
She looked up towards the road instead.
She softly spoke somebody's coming across the hill
All I could see was a horse running into the grassy field.

She stood to her feet with her hand across her forehead
With an eager look it wasn't the horse
somebody was coming instead.
As they got closer and closer to us
Our old dog began to make a fuss.

Momma and the man reached out their
arms to embrace each other
With such love she turned to me and
said this is your brother.
It was a hot steamy day in the sun
My brother came home. Momma called him the prodigal son.

Playmate

Writing this poem for you is hard for me
You were the very closest you see.
We grew up together as sister and brother
Obeyed daddy's rules also our mother's.

We chased each other as we played
And had lots of fun back in those days.
We were together the night mom got ill
Shared some memories and tears too if you will.

Watched you leave home and joined the service
Missed you like crazy which included some worries.
You served your time for your country and service too
Found you a girl for your heart so true.

Watched you move on with your life
Attended your wedding when you married your beautiful wife.
Struggles later came and you weren't doing so well
To see love and compassion in your heart even I could tell.

Flowers from your own garden you did save
You took them and planted them on mom and dad's grave.
I will continue to miss you each and every day.
Gone way too soon but *God* has his way.

Goodbye My Friend

We met when I was around the age of sixteen
Not in person but by telephone back then.
You would call and dad would hang up
He wasn't trying to be mean just did
not want to make a fuss.

Lonely he was during that time
Courting a younger woman and feeding her his line.
You continued to call even though you were being rejected.
He finally came around as you had previously projected.

In a dream momma came to him and blocked his path
Letting him know courting this younger
woman was enough at last.
I think he was worried about what I would say
As he continued to travel on his way.

Momma died many years after your husband did
There was nothing wrong with you putting in your bid.
You were the best thing that could have happened to my dad.
Every day I came home from school he
would be looking lost and sad.

Thank you for being in my dad's life and mine too
I could not think of another woman other than mom but you.
I missed him when he died at age seventy three
I will miss you. Now at the age 105 you are also free.

Once Upon A Time

Once upon a time it was you and me
A wonderful and loving relationship thought to be.
We walked in the warm late evening hour
The night ending with a sweet kiss under the water tower.

The moonlight shinning so beautiful and bright
Sometimes watching until the morning light.
The day you left me everything seem to change
No telephone call letters cards nothing with your name.

All the written letters I waited for
Each day I wanted to hear from you more and more.
With the times not hearing from you and
being up with a late night cry
Somehow along the way I learned like
many people love does die.

We must move on and choose our fate
Life is filled with a lot of give and take.
Even though we have drifted apart
I am sure you will be in my memories at
times but never again in my heart.

Dreams

Could dreams come true and be so real?
For it is you in my dream that I feel.
It is the gentleness of your touch
Keep me wanting you ever so much.

Seeing your little crooked grin
Thinking back to our last encounter then.
Holding me in your arms so tight
You made it special on our last night.

I can see you so good right now
All I need to do is touch you somehow.
The deeper and deeper in my dream I get
I do not want to wake up yet.

You are closer my dear though it seems
This is oh' so real not a dream.

Fallen Leaves

We have leaves that have fallen from our tree
Maybe this is the way *God* meant for it to be.
They originated from the roots at the beginning of its birth
Fell to the ground back on *God's* beautiful earth.
Fallen leaves one by one which we will never forget
Precious little leaves are now resting against *God's* breast.

Do Not Worry

When your troubles are too hard for you to bear
Do not worry' about your travels *God* will take you there.
When your friends are talking about you and turn their backs
Do not worry' because *God* has all the facts.

When you are on your job and in distress
This is when *God* is at his best.
Marriage has its ups and its down
Do not worry' because *God* will always be around.

When you say' I cannot deal with these problems of mine
He will also make everything just fine.
During your roads of travel' you might
have to pull over sometime.
Do not worry' *God* will be waiting at the finish line.

It Was Said

It was said' that dogs must learn
Unlike cats when they leave home they're likely will return.
Away the dogs go' sniffing everything else
He's barking and ruling instead of taking care of himself.

Let him out to exercise and have a chance to be free
Roaming around elsewhere and not where he should be.
He will stay out late and put his nose up someone else's tree
He should be at home spending time with me.

He's not satisfied' unless he is on the outside looking in
Trying to spend the rest of his days making
up with you and trying to be your friend.
Dogs must learn a lesson like the cats. When
they go out they should return.
They must keep in mind' they have no bridges to burn.

Thank you

Thank you for loving and protecting me in the past
Thank you for letting me recognize it at last.
Thank you for waking me up each and every day
Thank you for not passing me by and for coming my way.

Thank you for watching over me in the darkest of the night.
Thank you for helping me fight a good fight
Thank you for protecting me from all my troubles within
Thank you for accepting my night calls.
And being such a good friend.

Thank you from the bottom of my little heart
Thank you for all my breaks in life and for a good start.
Thank you for not being too busy and
listening to all my troubled problems
Thank you for not only stepping in also solving them.

Thank you for allowing me to keep in touch
Thank you for protecting and loving me so much.

My Stories

My stories that I have compiled
These poems have been written and filed.
Memories of the past I never could depart
They are special relationships from my heart.

Some of which your feelings maybe the same
Compile your memories and sign your name.
Get away to your special place and try to escape
Write your stories it is never too late.

He

He made me out of the darkest clay
He left me here on earth to stay.
He made me healthy beautiful and strong
He never once left me alone.

He gave me himself and became my friend
He also gave me a companion I can love within.
He gave me laughter joy and hope
He gave me love and a clean body without dope.

He protected me all the days of my life
He shielded me and later sent me a wife.
He supplied me with all my earthy needs
He humbled me. I stay prayerful and on my knees.

He gave me strong arms to reach to the heavens above
He gave me everything that also included his love.

Dare

I dare you to pray
I dare you to be educated
I dare you to have determination and overcome hardships
I dare you to love one another

I dare you to recognize that you were freed
I dare you to respect yourself and others
I dare you to break the family tree chain of improvement
I dare you to let your skin color or race
stand in your way with excuses

I dare you to get out of bondage
I dare you to overcome racism
I dare you to have hope
I dare you to have faith and trust in yourself and "*God*"

I dare you to move forward away from
the auction block of slavery
and possibly become the president of
the United States of America
I dare you.

Time

Time will always be maybe not for you or me
Time should be very well spent
To throw it away just doesn't make much sense.
Time is precious for us all
We shouldn't take it for granted for we
never know when we will fall.
Time is given to us by the All Mighty *God*.
Using it wisely simply will show him
the appreciation of his love.

Come Unto me

Jesus said; "suffer the little children come unto me".
He knew a better place for you to be.
Life may have been cut shorter than you would have liked
But Jesus made you humble got you ready for your flight.

We loved and enjoyed you while you were here on this earth
God said he had you in a better place.
Dispute any of Gods work we would not dare
This does not mean that we do not still care.

Someday my sweets no matter how much we try to avoid
We too will be coming home to be with you and the Lord.

Broken Wing

I dream of swimming on the lake's shore
Swim I cannot anymore.
My wing was broken on the right
Trying to get away from a fight.

I've enjoyed the cool waters especially in the spring
And the warmth from the sunlight it does bring.
Swam with my friends on those beautiful days
Quacking and communicating in our own ways.

Yes my broken wing is only for a while
Soon I will be swimming it is then I will smile.
For now I'll continue to burry my beak near my breast
Until I'm stronger and is rescued and back to my best.

When love do not love you

You love so hard thinking they love you
Heart feels all warm and butterflies in your stomach too.
We give our all in hopes for love in return
Once you have been bitten it is then you began to learn.

When love doesn't love you know it is not the same.
It does not only cause sleepless nights
but does cause you pain.
Sometimes you have to put a distance between
the love you thought was so true
A love that you once thought loved you.

Hidden Secrets

Oh Dear Molly Molly Lynne
She had so many secrets that went way back when.
Would she ever tell of her undesirable long past
Can Molly finally tell her kept secrets at last?

Molly was about 10 when a relative walked right in
While Playing with her doll which was her very best friend.
She never told a soul of what happened that day
People kept things quiet and what
happened they would not say.

For years and years she kept telling
herself tell the story Molly Lynne
Tell somebody if not your family just tell a friend.
Over and over in her mind tell no one in this town
For they would look upon you with a frown.

She could not tell her mom because it would hurt her so
To tell her dad the relative we would not see any more.
So what should she do she kept it in all these years?
Maybe put it in a tell all book and release her fears.

Should she comfort him and let him
know what he did was wrong
Does she go to her grave and leave this hidden secret alone?

Momma

Momma had six girls and boys of seven
When she died and went on to heaven
She left a husband sons sisters and brothers
And left some daughters later became mothers.

I can see her now so very clear
Heavenly wonderful and such a dear
Yes she was a loving woman so very wise
Out of all mother's she could have taken the prize

When I think back into the past
If she had it she would have given her very last.
She had this gentleness I couldn't seem to know
And a face she wore with such beauty and glow.

If you are at all anyway curious
Momma was a praying woman and very serious.
Even though she has died and gone away
I thank *God* for a momma that knew how to pray.

CPSIA information can be obtained at www.ICGtesting.com
Printed in the USA
LVOW13s1054110913

351856LV00001B/2/P